❀ MAXIMUM · GAGA ❀

LARA GLENUM

ACTION BOOKS
NOTRE DAME, IN 2008

Action Books
Joyelle McSweeney and Johannes Göransson, Editors
Jesper Göransson and Eli Queen, Art Directors
John Dermot Woods, Web Design

Action Books gratefully acknowledges the instrumental support
of the University of Notre Dame.

Learn more about us at www.actionbooks.org.

Or contact:
Action Books, Department of English, University of Notre Dame, 356 O'Shaughnessy
Hall, Notre Dame, IN 46556

Maximum Gaga

ISBN 13 978-0-9799755-3-0

Library of Congress Control Number: 2008933718

First Edition

Cover art: Mia Mäkilä
"The Others" (2007)

ACT I

THE NORMOPATH

MINKY MOMO SPEAKS OF NORMOPATHS

If you manage
to finagle   an orifice
out of my lubricious runts

a pink sugar deer
will pop out
of
my nacreous cumsacks

If you do finagle an orifice

I will probably
be the last to know about it

Who can feel anything in this weather

Suck the nectar
out of my swan bones
& jerk

O Normopath

When you speak to me
please address
my stuffed monkey first

In Springtime
the Normopath snoozles
among my ducts   warbling out a fancy idiocy

I should live a thousand years
with such a tumor

sez Minky Momo

Slipping eye-stalks into pre-formed grooves
the Normopath sees ghosts

& calls them fleshlord

This is the normal monster

POST ORIFICE

My normopath neighbor (a.k.a. "the Rooster")
started maling
          protoplasmic goo   into my bone pagoda
He began maling me spermatazoid valentines

He was going postal
He was maling all over me

In the male   I discovered coupons
                              for torch songs & a notice
for Mr. Humpty's Charity Ball
          In the male
I received an invitation to a language-den
of squealing verbs
                    tied to signposts
I received a finger
in my male-hole   I wagged it at my neighbor
          grinding his mewling pelt
into my feathered lawn

At the Post Orifice
                    I maled "the Rooster"
an invoice   for thirty-odd coxcombs
Mr. Oddcock, I said,
          You are invited for teeth & cookies

MINKY MOMO BEFORE THE JUDICIARY

I come from a long line of female seers who had visions of the Barbie-Christ. I attended various organizations, where we practiced collective assemblages of enunciation & anti-memory. In the Girl Scouts, we learned to cooperate by pulling harpoons out of each other's chests, by knitting platinum wigs & by competing for the "sauciest slit" badge. This brought in a very different regime of signs & even non-sign states.

When we started out
Mino told me
I am a stump-grubber
            & you are   *Vamp No. 7*

In the Museum of Accidents
I was shaking in my hole

I prepared for days of awe

PULCHRITUDE

Mino is hump-o-matic
Skeevy eye-candy   in the fuck factory
as only
      a grieving animal can be

a craquer
laquered with spooge

I twist his atrocious muscles   around my mouth
& skeletal legbones
His junk
dripping   off the polycursal walls

He sez
There is something jerking
in your ribcage

that is not a heart

It is cow-intestine white
& fibrous & gilled

I like my animals caged

sez
Minky Momo

So does the Normopath
mutters Mino

NORMALCORE

Beware the Normopath's   hobbity gaga
        when he performs normacles

on the cartilage-strewn
disaster site

                    when he performs
                        normacles
on the quivering   quail meat
spilling out
        of your grotslot

NORMALCORE

Beware the Normopath   knocking honey
into your facegrill

Crustyflaps
will crush your teeth into smiling

Give the Normopath a flabjob
&
watch his boomstick blow & break
open your eye

MINKY MOMO'S GAMINE MORPHOSIS

O Mountebank
Unhook your eye from my necrotic tissue
Unhook
your agitprop   hanging like gonads
          from the glass walls of my voluptorium

I sickle my momo   pickled in pink
& My teeth grow into sabers

          Oblige my momo monsters   sez Twinkie
Sink into my minky buns
& scream
          a line of creeping marine gastropods

I'm a full-blown slinkling
Volupt Volupt

I'm a maxi-momo minky
with no petticoats   With only my singing goat hair &
          rumpus-pod

So pop   your picture
of lolicon eyes
          & elfin school-girl ganglia
as I strip
my feral rods out of your momo crevices

as I get minky in the momodrome
A giant
creampuff   Agog & snogging wastrel spirits
          My genital crimes

speeding into creamzilla

No matter how far you lug your bizarro nodal mass
sez Minky Momo

You will never traverse yourself

Minkycore

I'm flexing my eye-pods
& feeling nasty
    I milk
     the Normopath
   & lube out   into a sea of congealed pig organs

     The woods laugh out a skin

My eye-pods break open &
A hundred other eyes
roll out

I'm filing down my hooves

I'm waiting for Mino
with a thousand open legs

MINKY MOMO ♥ MINO

☞Whip up my chickens
sez Minky
to Mino

(Mino was fucked for
via bovine machine)

I am ten virgins
guffawing in a labyrinth

listening to dainty bull hooves approach
like tinkling china

Bring it on
sez Mino
slicking back his curl-i-que horns

Open up   your bully gullet
sez Minky

My squealing gristle
& ramrod utensils
can hornswoggle meat out of any low eater

Mino   toggles my milk buds

          injects the miraculin
          & the sweetness inducers
go dead

MINKYCORE

My gold-winged clit   flits
                    through
          the aulde lang zone

      I am riding the rat out
      I am outing
              the mole
while you dangle your cockles in my custardy runtwort
My eye flaking
      like a cheap patina   into your rococo spasm

Me & my runts   coo & curdle
as your collapsible skeleton   squinches into my gullet

Fluids sluicing
          through the sky-tubes
          of our corkscrew-shaped genitals
     As we shed   our rosy lamb organs
across malignant Springs

My ratty lingua

                                 sound like the snapping

                of flightbones

as you do a cunning runtalingus

          to the sucking noises

                           of my blowhole victrola

Mino asks
So what's the difference
        between you & the Normopath

THE GOLDEN WIRES SINGING IN THE VEINS

Mino feeds at one end of me
The Normopath at the other

Angels eating glory out of my face
like ravenous curs

I'm half-in
half-out
of my blubber suit

Two feeding tubes dangling from my chest

My cunt a violent surge-hammer
in the mouth of the Redeemer

The animals my skin could not contain
are clanging through the hospital

Mammal Harm

I spread legs
& hooves & veiny nodes & twitching placenta paste
        onto my toast

        Pass the mammal harm
the Normopath said
reaching across the table   into my millennial wreckage
&
pulling out
        a bucketful of calf legs
You birthed a big one!   the Normopath crooned
draped in rope-like tendons

& a cartilaginous
party hat
        The herd thanks you
        for your compliance!
he squawked from across the room where he was
                        looping
                blood sausages like streamers
around the chandelier

but that was nothing
When the Normopath sprang out of my cake lobbing cow brains
        I knew we were done for

The creamery was indeed
closed

The devastating machines
were already groaning
&
pulling the new head
                              out of the intestinal casing
                of his face

CRASH SITE

Dribbling figgity
among   cream-slammed oinkers

the Normopath's piglicker

crushes into ham canyon

[The cherubim applaud wildly!]

Feminine Hygiene

When I contracted the "female disease"
the Normopath   said I would be manicured
in no time

but I knew I could never be manicured what with

        my wiry follicles & spitting fistulas
& Mino's
semen caked under my fingernails

All that grotty jiz crusting to sugar in my ass crevice

No acetylene virgincakes
waxing mannequin

& Later on my back
                my fangs slung over Mino's shoulder
      Everyone standing in the skybox could see
I was thrashing
malignancy   out of every oil-lubed pore

rancid & unyielding
No facemask made out of pantyliners   or baldifying grout

could cure me   of my monstrous frame

      or my unsightly cocklust
      which from the skybox appeared exactly like
a dancing turd

NORMALCORE

The Normopath says
Trade your face-socket in

for a wall of teeth

The Normopath says
Devour yourself

The Normopath whistles loudly
out of his eye-hole

Is pathologically normal

HYPNIC JERK

When cloud number 5287 skitters past
the grave bends
       & I escape
       A cross-eyed ghost

I descend on the metropolis
                 A sinister cream-puff
                 smearing beefsteak all over your millennial eye
My nerves   rattling their chainmail

      or so I told Mino
       while taking pipe
My cunt grew all sing-songy
amid his pettifogging miracles

& coughed out a deer head

It blinked &   said
Crack the fur-covered heavens   & forgo couture idols
Madame X

This is husky love
This is the real shitting out the carapace of the real

What is the real?
asks Mino

      A blubber field
      in which desire waves its prosthetic limbs

What is desire?

Language's cock valve

(The Normopath   was spilling

a singing chorus of fetuses
out of his face)

NORMALCORE

The Normopath
piles high
            his thousand prosthetic limbs

& stands atop
the monument

tweeking his nipples
splattered in birdshit

            You threw your genitals into my see
Minky Momo
told the Visual Oppressor

Will The Real Minky Momo
Please Step Forward

'This is not really happening,' Minky Momo muttered as the Normopath pulled her smock over her head. Beneath it, he discovered a laughing red fox. He unzipped its head. A Prussian soldier appeared. He unzipped it again. A grey squirrel costumed as a 19th C. czarina. Plunging his hand down beneath several layers of costume, the Normopath encountered a stretch of silky flesh. Mmm, he thought to himself, as soft as dandelions poking out of a dead soldier's custardy eye! He excavated the body. The graceful shoulders of a young man appeared, then the horns, then the belly & thighs, lavishly smeared with semen. '*So this is what you've been up to, o reprobate lover!*' the Normopath exclaimed, slyly stroking the boy's testicles & popping off his head. And o! Then the real Minky Momo did appear! Metal teeth gnashing, she flew out of the pile of costumes, her missing arm firing diamond bullets into the Normopath's cotton-stuffed, ammo-sucking head.

Minky Momo
stretches her labia around her body

like a cocoon
             & zips herself inside

& starts to holla

Guerilla This Guerilla That

I'm a peg-leg gladiatrix
Glad
to snog   cheap candy
from the suckhole

Glad to pop the badly-wigged boy

Glad to be arachnoid
& spent

My peg-leg snapping
My layers of porpoise fat   unfurling like a galleon banner

I am going down
on my trick knee

      I am demanding   a historical reenactment
      of Seven Cunt Mary's seizing
the walloped hill

      O war-time taxidermist

My bajingo is ring-a-linging
           I am coddling my mincemeat
        into a retro set of vibrating clouds

There are a variety of ways to become a monster. What is "unnatural." I am as much a Normopath as Poseidon's trannie mermaids.

When the Queen denatured herself & put on the simulacrum, she became the real. In a maze of mechanical muscles, she found unspeakable cock at bargain basement prices. Then she could no longer be digested or in other ways consumed.

There are a variety of ways to become a monster. The first is to engage in artifice.

In making simulacra, we do not displace the real, we manufacture it. All denizens of our kingdom enjoy being strapped into machines & balled by charismatic macrofauna.

Artifice may be the road to hell, but it is the only road that doesn't end there, forging on to crueler paradises.

✦ ACT II ✦

MEAT OUT
OF
THE EATER

CAST OF CHARACTERS

Minus	*King of Catatonia*
Queen Naked Mole Rat	*A fetishist*
The Visual Mercenaries	*A secret order*
King Minus's Daughters	*A Hysteric machine*
Ded	*A Schizophrenic machine*
Icky	*A Paranoiac machine*
The Surgeon General	*By royal appointment*
Poseidon's Trannie Mermaids	*Chorus*
The Queen's Stunt Double	*A relic of hysteria*
The Miraculating Machine	*A Desiring-machine (a simulacrum)*
Mino	*Lodged in the Traumadome*
The Traumadome	*A maze of muscles*

Setting: The Kingdom of Catatonia.

SCENE I

INSIDE
THE ROYAL CHAMBER

King Minus had a secret pigsuit

In it   he hid his face
made entirely of teeth

His other face ran on rails
down to the harbor

to eye-fuck the mermaids
like any old Normopath

Queen Naked Mole Rat
was his eighth queen

didn't keen to pigsuit

wouldn't be hobblesucked
by that curly little tail

The royal chamber
was fashioned entirely from teeth

In it   the king stood naked
in his pig suit

calling forth the Visual Mercenaries

Come to beautiful Catatonia & bleed off our vision

We in Catatonia
are suffering from a surplus of vision

When the Visual Mercenaries
burst into
the royal chamber

King Minus lay face-down on his bed of teeth
pressing his toothy face
into his toothy pillow

Alas we are doomed
he hiccupped

giggling inside
like a runty hyena
with a stomach full of schoolgirl

SING SING!
[Song of the First Visual Mercenary]

Va voom! went the Minx, squirreling his dogma into my squeezebox. We were in Sing Sing tattooing each other's cornea with anti-state propaganda & birthing Ziploc bags full of mice. At the cantine, salt-caked chandeliers swayed over dancing bears in porcelain helmets. Me & the Minx were hinky-pinky. During rinky-dink hijinxs, diamonds flashed out of our head-wounds. O Heads of State, beware our carnelians! Our laboratory aesthetics! Our super-vixenated language engines & coochy-coo histories that fly straight into the open maw of the apocalypse! O Squires of Sonnets, jettison your tired kidneys & metal pants & lie down on our operating table! Let us extract bright abominations out of the star-shaped hole in your face! Let us graft you squalling to our industries of light!

:: ORACLE ::

While eating the Queen

the Visual Mercenaries
declared her body to be the site of revolution

THE SITE OF REVELATION
WILL LATER BE TOSSED OUT AS PIGSHIT

King Minus got screwed
in the eye-socket
by the Visual Mercenaries

One coochie-pop &
his vision was aborted

They impregnated him with "coochie sight"
& all manner of   conceptual abstractions

I am a miracle!
he declared

training his blind coochie gaze
on his daughters

frilled out in pink meringue
& hanging from the ceiling

like oscillating mobiles

Is this a museum?
asked one of the Visual Mercenaries

SONG OF KING MINUS'S DAUGHTERS
[To be sung "frilled out in pink meringue & hanging from the ceiling"]

Mama, mama! I'm a steamship! she cried/ spine forking/&
bald as a baby mouse/
This was later recorded/ by the "good doctor"
        w/rechargeable fangs

The four-legged/
incarnation convulses/ on the bare floor/ Hemiplegic/ The sister
reduced to its spherical belly/ radiating two pelvises/

        "O my sweet/captive amputee!"

Right thigh ends abruptly/ mid-air!/ The table leg wears/
a matching boot!

        :: How Are Girls Different? ::

        :: Where Do I Come From? ::

Notice/ the undeveloped pudenda/
& juvenile hairbrows

Notice:/ two are "on all fours"/ in a clonic spasm/
in striped stockings/
Think:/ What do I deserve?
Think:/ The fused torsos/ of Siamese twins/ "Posed in/
                                sinister narrative tableaus!" :
                domestic interiors/basement/hayloft/or forest

Cephalopod (n.): species having a well-developed head
surrounded by tentacles, viz. *scuttlefish, octopus*

Striped Stockings + Boots/ reappear/ to confront the Colonel/
"Altogether stripped/ of flesh & *deathly!*"/ quoth the frightened chambermaid
"Stomach carved open"/
Their visceral membranes/ draped over
their arm/
"like a mink stole!"/

Now who's/ the Fancy-pants?

Press any nipple/ to make the four breasts rotate/
on the neck-pedestal!/
To make the legs splay/ "as if in a fit!"

(The Chimney!)/ (appears stage left!)/ (spewing white vapors!)
Spewing "magic kits"/ Easter eggs/ Cat's-eye marbles!

Lying in a wet ditch/ in the parlor/ a hemianesthetic:/ knock-kneed legs/
peek-a-boo transparent skirts/ + A glass eye/
Glue dripping down/
her marble nerves

tightly bound with string – /
"A pale lump/ of trussed meat":/

Keep in a cool place

48

PROCLAMATION OF THE VISUAL MERCENARIES

Citizens of Catatonia!

Now that our nation is under siege, we should all take refuge in Maximum Gaga. We should all beg refuge in Maximum Gaga & its glorious excesses, yes, we should all beg as we cross the border gripping bags of our own organs in our teeth, fleeing the terror. We should unfurl Maximum Gaga like a banner as we stream into the forbidden city where all our hopes lie, as well as a handy store of detonating devices, a slew of candy-mouthed surgeons & certain laryngitis.

What have you done with all your words & gaudy language-hats? Ask Maximum Gaga, that oracle of oracles! Maximum Gaga says: you have been supremely swindled. You have not been severally penetrated by sublime linguistic prongs, not even once. Language has refused to abduct you, refused to shove you bodily into ferocious states in which your brain would luxuriate in fields of wiggity-wack. Language has dismissed you without even a healthy romp in the gravy mines.

How to rectify this, o dog of language? How to rectify your losses at the hands of your own tongue? Run headlong into Maximum Gaga! Run, now that your own poor words have been crammed back into your torso like guinea pig carcasses & greasy red clouds, now that you face certain doom from all quarters! Seek sanctuary in Maximum Gaga!

Bite down on the iron axis of submission! Submit to all great powers, but submit first to Maximum Gaga & its infernal complex of arms dealers & linguistic sewers! Submit to have the central nervous system flensed out of your poems & strung up like Christmas lights around the sublunary city!

O vowel-laden citizens, let us erect monuments on the site of your gravest misfortunes, celebrating the victory of the cage! The glorious cage of language from which we never hope to escape!

When Minus became pregnant
the Queen
zipped on her carnage suit

She knew she was no mother
to abstractions

Ultraclown

O my prosthetic soul

My cadaverine joy
My chiming weaponry & the puny bodies that carry it

Face-down in the ultraclown
I'm caramelizing
my joy-oil
& smearing it on my hump-pistons

I'm wall-eyed
in the shooting gallery

O my eye-
popping Normopath

     Spare me
     your exotic shame-wig
& shrunken brain-stem   Spare me
your white-face   dripping like curds
     out of your mouth-hole

O the houses of sorrow
you build with your eye-beams

your clown armies advancing
into the folds of my industrial skirts

HEAVY INDUSTRY IS LOCATED IN THE LACTATING BODY

I am the mother of the state!
Minus declared

after he had 18 breasts
surgically implanted on his torso

with a tube running from each breast
to every city

His milk even ran beneath the streets

in all of the rat-clogged sewers

[INTERMEZZO!]

A BURLESQUE IN A SEWER.

[The Queen enters wearing her carnage suit. The stage floor is piled high with Minus's milk-tubes, which drip ominously off the edge of the stage, spilling out onto the audience. The Queen's meringue daughters dangle from the ceiling, farting out nightingales.]

QUEEN *[looking ruefully over her shoulder]*:

Stupid hominids!
Vision is its own abortifacient!

The eye hollows out the genitals

Nothing can grow where the eye reigns

Not even in Catatonia

I must make of my carnage
a miraculating machine

MINUS [*barking*]: I am the great artificer!

DED [*irked*]: I am the great artificer!

CHORUS OF TRANNIE MERMAIDS [*warbling*]: We are the great
artificer!

[*The ceiling of the stage is crammed with naked men whose bodies rotate as cogs in a great
machine. Steam billows out of all their orifices.*]

THE COG-MEN [*shouting in unison*]:

The Queen
is the great artificer!

[*The cog-men go all bubbly and sport erections. Leaping down from the ceiling, they do a can-
can. In their navels, entire insect empires come and go.*]

[The Surgeon General enters, toting a megaphone. He leans out over the audience.]

SG: But who was THE GREAT ORIFICER?

[*A lone spotlight illuminates a charming domestic scene in a house made entirely of teeth. The furniture is made of squealing pigs. The Queen sits on the couch, her ribcage cranked open to display nine tea-cups dangling on hooks. In each tea-cup, baby rats are continually born and tumble out of her body to scavenge on the floor.*]

MINUS [*frazzled & nursing a milkpup, shouts to Queen*]:

Get back into your orifice

& close the damn door!

[*The milkpup grows into a thousand-eyed apocalypse.*]

To commit artifice is a crime
punishable by dread

To commit orifice is a crime
punishable by mirth

[Ded & Minus walking arm & arm in the sewer.]

DED: A central component of maintaining & reproducing social order
       is the management of women

             The primary strategy for the control of women
             is their public representation

DED: The Queen's carnage suit
       must be converted
       into a docile cow

[Exuent.]

[The Queen's Stunt Double enters, holding up the Queen's latest decree:]

The Great Orificer & the Great Artificer will commingle
in the Miraculating Machine!

[Mid-stage, she stops and does the jig known as "brushing the ham." While handling the wily ham, she becomes infected and marvelously deforms.]

The Body is the Inscribed Surface of Events!

A Volume in Perpetual Disintegration!

The Body is Always Under Siege!

[*A great cymbal crash & a smoke puff & the Miraculating Machine appears mid-stage!*]

[*All players return to the stage and begin vying to be the first to enter the machine.*]

[*The Bull enters, smirking. All fall to the ground. The Bull begins playing the human organ long and low.*]

[*Inside the machine, the human organ wheezes out its spasmodic calcified joy.*]

SCENE II

IN THE
PORNOTOPIARY

King Minus kept the little white bull to see what his wife would do. King Minus kept the little white bull for hot young Icky to ride.

ZOOPHILIA

King Minus   traveled to Phonecia

leaving mother
Icky & Ded

lost in a maze of muscles

Icky &
Ded
spread out on the bed

flaunting their golden hamhocks

SCOPOPHILIA

Icky & his school-boy minions
race past
        flapping wax wings

Seed-pods dangling
against slavish thighs

My eye-pods raving

I want to wrap my membranes
around all of them
& have an organism

[QUEEN: Icky's face was the original sublime event. Basting
in my own oologic juices, I was sore afraid. After copulation,
I was merely sore.]

DED'S TREATISE ON THE MIRACULATING MACHINE

Copulating is not just becoming as one, or even two, but becoming as a hundred thousand.

Desire (re)produces reality. Desiring-machines are the site of that (re)production. All desire is mimetic.

The Miraculating Machine stands outside all mimesis & therefore, outside all desire.

[*The Queen approaches the Miraculating Machine & climbs inside.*]

The Cow That Ded & Icky Built

I'm all decked out
in decoy cow

      I'm ogling the stomping white bull
I'm salivating   & flexing my anemic gonads
I'm starving for the old

Hitch & Ball

      My four fake stomachs ajar
      My queenly coos
          full of tiny dollhouse furniture

The beastie cranks out   a tenderloin
My cowhide flapping nervy with cooch

A small pop   & ah!
An ultra-mechanical   maze of muscles
to boondoggle a monster

THE BRIDE MACHINE PRODUCES CATATONIC STATES

I am Vamp No. 7
I speak inflected with cow

My face-hood
is evolving into the mascot for Stump Village

I am an oracle in reverse   maiming whose shrimpy words

You are a cow-word
The dolorous cow clit flitters its two sets of gold wings
& spits in your left eye

The Marquise's cow-ghost drags her crotch across the parlor
Thump thump

& the night
sprouts an oracular carbuncle
to jaw out   my cream-swollen chumpy

[A Pull-Out Centerfold of Icky]

Icky   (a Visual Oppressor)
renounced his status

In an efflorescence of disability
he plucked out his arms

& strapped on
prosthetic wings

:: The chorus of able bodies coos! ::

THE SIGN OF THE GOAT
[Icky's Song]

I saw myself lying spread-eagle on a slab of whale blubber   :   egg-cream
custard dripping down my thighs   :   I saw myself wearing a necklace

of cow hearts   :   The inflated ventricular membranes exploding
one by one : I saw myself in pig-skin & rhinestone helmet   :   pulling

the stitching out of my chest to reveal   :   a veil of red
rubber tubes   :   I saw myself wearing stilettos of meat

& laughing : I saw myself dressed in pink-eye   & tumors : modeling
the latest vivisection device :   :   I saw myself lying on a gurney

surrounded by   deer in white jackets   :   My spine being pulled out my
asshole   :   like a string of diamonds   :

ICKY, THE PARANOIAC MACHINE

I am Icky
I fell into the see

when Poseidon's trannie mermaids
got hold of me

I was dislodged
from
all mythology

[Song of Poseidon's Trannie Mermaids]

Come to us
in your carnage suit   Snookums
& we'll blow your sea-junk into the aquamarine rollers
            & set you
yelping astride
triple-pronged Poseidon

Drowned men   marooned in pornotopic jaws
          of giant clams
dial us   for a wiggy bit of caviar
& split-tailed monster mischief

MY ROCOCO OVO
[Song of the Queen of the Trannie Mermaids]

My rococo ovo
are trilling & pervy
                        in curly cream clouds
            I strap on my pink plastic regatta
            & pirates
lay their eggs in the crannies of my teeth

Heave-ho
the vibratron
Me & the Squid are gang-planking
            the First Mate
            We're grinding him down to aromatic stubble &
cum bubbles
            We do the "moisto shuffle"
            into the sea-tubes
wagging our gyroscopes at the armies of the sea

Yo ho ho
I wave my pegleg
            at sea-monsters
& drag my tiny uterus   behind the sloop
The Squid
is a sea-curio machine
                        of speedy nudes
            & other jolly trinkets scraped off the sky's libertine tongue
            I finger
the sperm whale
            & we cream barnacles into a nautical dictionary
We jettison
our scurvy tentacles
            into tender squalls of the zygote-laden sea

SECRET & SUPPRESSED DOCUMENTS

Pelvis Impersonator

[Statement delivered by the Surgeon General
to the Royal Academy of Science]

Esteemed Colleagues –

Females who are promiscuous tend to evolve high sperm counts & large testes. They live in caves, lose their eyes & their color. Whether they live in Rwanda or Romania, they're a pallid, blind lot, the troglodytes. Their pelvis is a complicated affair that comes complete with a pair of long spines. Some have also lost their hind legs. All that's left of their pelvis is a lopsided bone, smaller on the right than on the left: the ghost of pelvis past.

Pelvic loss is much less common than armor loss. Some of the invaders carried this rare version with them.

Let's turn now to the ghostly pelvis. Some of the females are switched on everywhere except the pelvic region & the pelvis doesn't grow. They have crushed faces & abnormal pituitaries that cause them to die young. Intriguingly, they also have reduced forelimbs. Left to their own devices for four & a half billion years, what would happen?

Here, I've focused on one particular version of the evolutionist's dream. But there are many others: the spiky pelvis, the evolved female foregut, rows of bony plates. Marooned & isolated, these invaders subsist, the exits of the lakes closed.

A Cock & Bull Story
[The testimony of the Queen]

The Visual Mercenaries injected the stuffed monkey
into me
through the puncture point
The shunt in my stomach

They dug it out again
with a hook
& named it Roscoe

Buried it again

then dug the shrunken fetal king out of the red marshes
Out of the soft bowl of bone
They dressed it in lacy knickerbockers

& worshipped it

Only then did the Captains of Industry proclaim me
their "truest ballerina & heir"

A black plastic bag   in which a porcelain uterus swam
                                       under the steam

        of its golden propeller

FAMILY PLANNING
[The testimony of the Queen]

The Surgeon General
had a slit   implanted in the middle of his chest

He nested it in a doily
of Spanish lace   His "most magnificent slit"
                    wore a 16th C. ivory ruff

The swans honking
among his organs puked up trash & a case of syringes

When I saw his cosmetically-implanted slit
I snapped out a shriveled rib
& shook it at him

causing his slit to bulge

            & his false tentacular udders
coaxed me
into a hospital bed
                    I poked at his slit with my IV stand
                                It snarled uncouthly
                        in its Spanish ruff
& spat out his official state seal

Fertility
[The testimony of the Queen]

I hung my ovaries over the door of the homestead
& invited the Surgeon General
into my parlour

His assistants hooked me up to the "weeping machines"

The machines wore rabbit ears
& spoke in code
as they harvested my sense-organs

My eye-guns were removed

& the machines pumped cream
into my every orifice
with rubber hoses

until I was dribbling cream out of my eyesockets
Cream hemorrhaging out of my nostrils & ears

A siren wailed
as they attached the silver prongs to my undercarriage
& cut the wires   to my peripheral defense system

Each part of my body
was ultimately alarmed

The vagina is found in divers Manners, and with divers Ornaments. Many of them provide the finest Articulations, and Foldings, for the Wings to be withdrawn, and neatly laid up inside. Occasionally the petiole embraces the branch from which it springs. The Empalement, which commonly rises out of a membranous vagina. The embryo dracunculi, it is said, will quit the body of the vaginaless parent worm. Sometimes soldiers lie together like teeth crouching in a perfect labia. The fibers of their leg muscles are then distinguished by crenellated or adipose septa, as by so many peculiar vaginæ. The vagina's variants in North America alone are innumerable; the most important being the crushing entrance to heaven, snapping doors.

THE HYSTERIC MACHINE PRODUCES NERVESUITS
USED IN STATE EXECUTIONS

O Charity

Minus's daughters made nervesutits
for death row inmates
to enhance their deathwork

They also made a nervesuit for the wilting executioner

When the Visual Mercenaries were executed
for crimes against the state
Minus's daughters sewed pig bones into the shoes of the spectators
& sold
blood pudding in disposable cups

The spectators raved
that this greatly enhanced their experience

THE DOUBLE IS THE SITE OF TERROR

The beastie was skinking around in the pink
with fidgety feelers
He was
crooking around in the pink   for some goatspank

In my silky porkpot
he was beserking around

that queen-mounted beastie

with his wheedling automata
& I was
gob-smacked
That beastie   He horned around
in the theme park of my most mechanical flesh

& I was goblinesque
& moony
with thousand-pound swaggering lips

my brillie wagging
loud & outright

& I was no one's freaking identical then

THE QUEEN'S STUNT DOUBLE ON NATIONAL TV

A: Who hired you?
Q: The Queen. At least at first. Later, I came on my own terms.

Q: What exactly was your job?
A: I was the stand-in for the Queen during all the sex scenes. She never did her own sex scenes.

Q: Were you satisfied with the compensation?

A:

Desire in any form
leaves you crawling into rude machines
leaves you hitched   inside a hideous skinbag

for little or no pay

[The Queen's Stunt Double pauses dramatically before the cameras.]

A:

Wrenching
the bull-neck back

Prying open the massive gullet
with my muzzleloader

to insert
my metal leg   & putrid crinolines

My fleshy nude amasses upon   the
Gargantuan organ
          No pastoralia but

push push

The landscape dissolving in air-strikes
of bird shit

The Miraculating Machine

The bit entered my zygomatic bone, pinning me to the machine. The sex cylinder was issuing nectar onto the metal drums. I pressed my hide to the beast's mouth & milk issued from the metal drums & rotating sparks were set onto the burgeoning field. I said, 'This is the apotheosis of virginity.' Blood appeared on my teeth. The retinal syrup poured out of the beast's eye & onto my electrical stripping.

I walked out onto the sea, the sea like a skinned membrane. I curled up beneath it, a hairy pupa. Inside the pupa, I grew a face of solid pearl.

When the whole city
was placed under quarantine

Ded's Second Treatise on Simulacra

There is a kind of primal pleasure, of anthropological joy in cows, a kind of brute fascination unencumbered by aesthetic, moral, social or political judgments. It is because of this that I suggest they are immoral.

If our modern cows fascinate us so much it is not because they are sites of meaning & representation – that would not be new – it is on the contrary because they are sites of the *disappearance* of meaning & representation.

Cows are thus sites of a fatal strategy of denegation of the real & of the reality principle.

Thus perhaps at stake has always been the murderous capacity of cows, murderers of the real.

THE SCHIZOPHRENIC MACHINE PRODUCES BRIDES
(IS EAU ET GAZ
ON ALL FLOORS)

Ded though a confirmed bachelor

still managed to produce
over 1,000 miraculating machines

which he called in private
"bride machines"
("cows inside cows" he quipped)

& one bull costume
for himself

to wear on formal occasions

(Ded's schizoprenia was well-documented
in the annals of the Surgeon General)

❈ SCENE III ❈

INSIDE THE TRAUMADOME

Dear Father

The red weather is laying its eggs in my torso The eggs of
amnesia   The red weather is flexing its terrible gills

The red weather is running radio wire through the holes
in my cheeks & giving me a plastic jaw filled with soft
decaying language

My sockets are draining onto the heath of diseased signs

I need a non-sign state A state not lined with corpses   I
feel the machine between my legs shift & bulge

Dear Mother

I bent mine eye-sleeves around "bad-willing I" to believe in your act of milk-violence The horse of wooden laughter forms the skin of my eye-sleeves You break open & insert hundreds of other eyes I with thousand open legs expect

Dear Minky

I have folded mine eye-muffs around "the defective-disposed one" My breach of the opened eye-muffs slides the switch of emergency to the outside My role is mimetic I am outside the desire of all I "then-and-therefore" & "with a thousand little legs" preview

Dear

Of all the ones with wooden skin & Of all the hundreds of other eyes Only my desire mimics your filed-down legs

WELCOME TO THE TRAUMADOME

Amazed of muscles
Mino sits
inside the polycursal machine

plucking his one pinking organ

to the sound
of snapping necks

The virgins who find him
say
he is failing quickly now

O CATATONIA
[A national anthem]

Minus
is a national eye-con
      The chandeliers lurch above the crash site
           & a fetus crawls out of
the star-shaped hole in my face

Beneath the eye-con's skin tent   sublime atrocities
         litter the crash site
      The squealing nest of fetal pigs
raises a monument   out of infected organs & chandelier glass
out of stringy tendons
& cunt nodes

What is desire in Catatonia
      Where I am a cunty pirate
lurching   down the gangplank

[*flourish of piccolos*]

Where we are all going down
in a submarine of dried meat

[*flourish of piccolos*]

Where mercenaries
strap on white stiletto boots &   crime wigs
          & march down
                        our nerve-strings

          sending lewd valentines
to the Captains of Industry

[*tuba fanfare*]

O Island of Catatonia
The ocean   is a series of nesting dolls

& in the final doll
the juicy morbid national eye

Dear Minky
I was fucked for

Mother was no Normopath
couldn't settle for bullocks

had to translate
flesh   into traumadome

          had to have
          full horn

She did not repeat
the normal monster

She did not repeat

SONG OF THE BULL

I'm a chittering knot
of raw
pigeon meat   My needlebones poking out the holes
     in my cheeks
     I bust out of my restraint bonnet
& shake
my catgut & whalebone buttons
          I shake my perfumed piles of gooseflesh
     down to stubble
     &
     a burnt-out leash

STATEMENT MADE BY THE BULL TO THE INQUEST

Q: When the queen was discovered twitching inside the machine, how did you respond?

A: Like I cared. By that time, all of Catatonia was using the machine on the sly. It had become quite fashionable. Two palace guards helped people sneak in at night for a go.

THE BULLY MACHINE

What was miraculating. One could not see the mechanical cow for all the fucking. Costume to costume, they lay. The bull was a simulacrum with no passengers inside. The mechanical cow was a body without organs. The balling was grand.

Interview with the Queen on National TV

Q: Is it really necessary to make such abominations?

A: It is absolutely necessary to make such abominations.

EXCERPT FROM
THE NOTEBOOKS OF THE QUEEN
[DURING HER DELICATE PERIOD OF CONFINEMENT]

GAGA SAGA

I trained my meat gazer
onto the sperm field   & the babies came

One fell out of my wooden hand
                    Another popped out of my stinkeye
& came back
dragging animal parts

        One smoked candy cigarettes
behind the wardolly   & burned my effigy
Another ate
        pickled umbilicals
& drove a plastic toy uterus around the graveyard

I ran through a field of snapping cocks
I wanted to trade my birth tuba   for an ambulance

I wanted to seal   these summer runts
in bags of custard
& carry them through the long war in my clanging torso

CRUNK SUNK IN THE MEAT JUNK

My frothing hunks   of fetal paradise
drain out
the back of my gristle day
        Stewing the landscape
                  like a monkey basting in its own sperm

I store my jewels in the false back of a mammal
My hollow fish eyes
        filled with egg salad
        My hollow legs   full of fetus-salad sandwiches

Curb the hunger of the masses
with my blue-veined   fish cavities

The laughing fetal mob
can't get enough of   boiled egg eyes
     or
       the whips that fall on the piles of cast-off muscles
badgering the dead

They are filling my paradise lung
with lungfish
& kettlefish   & kettles chock full of virgin cock

The eye-red lamb leaking whipped eggs across the parlor
The books
turning into feathered holes

The fetal mob trundles around tossing crusty jewels
       into the curdled lake
Tomorrow they will ride the mammals down into the sewers

They will chew the fur off paradise

Tenderloin

I attach my eartrumpet
to
the wardolly
       & My girly-gills grow frilly
       with wormeyes

       I hear the soldiers in the next room over
checking my frill-cage for sea-monkeys

I take a snack
off the cock-trolley
       & The soldiers roll their wooden eyes across the floor
       I jiggle my waste
& the rotters shoot out of my flaw-doll
I straddle their shiny magazines
of ammo
       & wooden eyes halt
at a hemline

The soldiers are coaxing my chandeliers
into the belly   of the wardolly
       & The sea-monkeys come on like cavalry
waving their tenderloins
             I shoot my crumpet
             into their smellies
       & babies drop out
of my bombazine
I grow into a girly empire
which is a mutant foe & willy nilly sirloin

soldiers buried in acres of burnt-out flesh

PURLOIN

Sir Loin's loins are gristle-heavy & combustible. They rebuke all polyps, medusas, fistulas costumed as men. I am not a "norm." Sir Loin's loins leak ribeye, leak lamb legs. Sprouting lamb legs, the loins gambol & cast their neural nets over my eggmeat.

The empire breeds at the front of the soldier's trousers. Slice open the five-star eggmeat & lift out an esophagus. Attach wooden eyes to esophagus with wire or tendon.

Swaddle & feed. Plates of cuckoo milk will grow the bones out nice & long. Will grow the bones into electric cattle prods.

CUNTBOX AUXILIARY

Despite my glassed-in I
& my lamb   in the gap
        I am gross

A non-crystalline rigid of poor optical quality

I am deep in the fungal house
& I am gross
up to my occipital horn

Can you make contact
with the insides of the animal

The Crystal Palace is full of Visigoths

The lecture
        given by the "fetal haint in rouge & boots"
was widely attended
by dilettantes
                posed in classic tableaus
        such as "The Glazier's Death"

In the Great Exhibition Hall
I displayed   my slime-black braincombs
        & fisted a garden gnome

At the Ladies' Cotillion   I wore specula
dangling from my frontal lobes
& served skunk ovaries   on larded-up crackers

I said   Dahling   Shut your cuntbox
I was still veering
to obey
                my not-owned form

Bio

Lara Glenum is the author of two books of poetry: *The Hounds of No* (Action Books, 2005) and *Maximum Gaga* (Action Books, 2008). She lives in Athens, GA.

Thanks to the editors of the following journals in which many of these poems initially appeared: *Action, yes, Octopus, jubilat, Conduit, Soft Targets, Fourteen Hills, Typesetter, Coconut, New American Writing, Columbia Poetry Review* and *Miposias*.

I would also like to thank Josef Horacek, Danielle Pafunda, Johannes Göransson, and Joyelle McSweeney for their invaluable feedback and support.

This book paraphrases or appropriates the work of Mary Russo, Deleuze & Guattari, Michel Foucault, and Jean Baudrillard in certain places.